Mendes DeSolla

A catechism of the Jewish religion

Mendes DeSolla

A catechism of the Jewish religion

ISBN/EAN: 9783337259136

Printed in Europe, USA, Canada, Australia, Japan

Cover: Foto ©Lupo / pixelio.de

More available books at **www.hansebooks.com**

A

CATECHISM

OF THE

JEWISH RELIGION,

BY

J. MENDES DE SOLLA,

Head Master of the Religious Schools of the Congregations
Emanu-El and Sherith Israel, San Francisco.

———•———

SAN FRANCISCO:
BACON & COMPANY, BOOK AND JOB PRINTERS,
No. 536 Clay Street, below Montgomery.
1871.

PREFACE.

That the youth of our community is especially in need
of religious and moral instruction, seems to me a fact
hardly to be disputed or doubted; and it appears equally
as evident that in order to impart such instruction meth-
odically and profitably, a manual to be used as a class-
book in our religious schools is indispensable. We have
no such book, and, as far as I am aware, there is none to
be had which will fully answer our purpose. It is true,
several catechisms and manuals for the religious instruction of Jewish scholars have from time to time been issued
by some of our ministers and teachers, but these are either
out of print or unsuitable. I shall not venture to criticise
in particular the productions of my predecessors in that
field, many of whom surpass me in ability and learning;
but it seems that the high attainments of some of these
authors rendered them unable to stoop to the level of the
comprehension of young students, and the consequence
is that the ideas laid before them are often abstruse; the
answers to the questions put to them too lengthy and diffi-
cult. The Board of the Religious School of the Congregation Emanu-El of this city, aware of this deficiency,
requested me, about three years ago, to prepare a catechism for the use of their school. This request I readily
complied with, and for upwards of two years and a-half
these lessons have been taught to the classes under my
immediate tuition, and I dare say with very fair results;
though I labored under the disadvantage of being obliged

to dictate the lessons to the scholars, requiring them to write the questions and answers for study at home.

In the month December of last year the congregation Sherith Israel, of this city, having determined to establish a religious school for the children of its members, honored me with the appointment of principal of their new institution; and with the approval of the Superintendent and Board of Directors of said school, I introduced the catechism there also.

The usefulness of the book having thus extended over the two largest Jewish schools in our city, I determined to publish the same; and I now venture to lay it before the public, trusting that my humble labors may in a measure contribute to the promotion of good morals and the knowledge of the true principles of religion among the youth of our community not only, but that its utility may extend even to schools outside of this city and state. As the lessons it contains touch upon neither extreme orthodoxy nor ultra reform, but teach only such principles and duties of our religion as are adopted and practiced by our people generally, the book has met the approval of those even who differ in their views on some minor points of our religious tenets and observances, and has consequently been accepted as a manual for the highest classes in the schools of the different congregations.

As to the intrinsic merit of the work I shall say nothing, but leave teachers and ministers, and those whose province it may be to see to such matters, to judge for themselves.

It will be observed that the lessons are divided into two parts, treating first of *Principles*, then of *Duties*, which suggested itself to me as the most convenient and natural division of the principal subject. I have especially aimed at conciseness and clearness, and have endeavored to lay before the young learner only such things as are most important for him to know, without overburdening either his mind or his memory.

I am indebted for some corrections and suggestions of improvement to Mr. John Swett, Deputy Superintendent of Public Schools in this city, who kindly revised the work with me; also, to Rev. Dr. A. Messsing and Mr. D. D'Ancona, to all of whom I hereby express my gratitude for their valuable aid.

That this unpretending little volume may be the means of improving the mind and heart of our young co-religionists; and that almighty God may send his blessing upon it, is the Author's heartfelt desire.

SAN FRANCISCO, June 21st, 1871.

INDEX.

FIRST PART.
RELIGIOUS DOCTRINE.

SECOND PART.
PRACTICAL RELIGION.

FIRST PART.

RELIGIOUS DOCTRINE.

FIRST LESSON.

RELIGION AND ITS OBJECT.

Q. What does religion teach us?

A. Religion teaches us *first*, the existence of a Creator and his attributes; *second*, our duties toward God and man; and *third*, what we are to expect from the performance or neglect of such duties.

Q. What is the great object of religion?

A. To make man moral and virtuous, and consequently content and happy in this life and hereafter.

Q. How does it make a man content and happy in this life?

A. It gives us the assurance that there is a great Being who is wise and good, who cares for us and protects us, and who does everything for our good. When adversity comes upon us, religion affords us the consolation that it proceeds from God, who wisely directs it so ; and when prosperity meets us, we enjoy it·the better when we know that it does not come to us by chance, but as the gift of a loving Father.

Q. And how does it make us happy hereafter ?

A. The duties which religion prescribes and the principles it teaches, being all calculated to improve our mind and character, it cannot fail to make us better if we follow its precepts. Thus religion purifies and ennobles our soul, and makes it fit to enjoy the presence and glory of God in a future life.

Q. Why could we not be happy without having any religion ?

A. Because there is a natural inclination in man for religion. Feeling our human weakness, we naturally look up to a more powerful Being ; knowing that we must die,we are inclined to hope and look for something beyond this life, and more lasting than what this world can yield.

Q. How does man's natural inclination for religion show itself ?

A. In all ages and in all parts of the world, certain forms of worship have been introduced; and in the absence of true religion, man has invented systems of false religion.

Q. Could not their false religion produce to them the same happiness, when they did not know any better?

A. No. Experience has shown that idolatry and religion of man's own invention led them to the greatest vices and cruelties. Therefore, God, in mercy to his creatures, revealed to them what is right and good.

SECOND LESSON.

THE GENERAL PRINCIPLES OF RELIGION.

Q. What are the principal points upon which all systems of civilized religion are based?

A. The belief in the existence of a God, in revelation, and in future reward and punishment.

Q. What do we mean by the existence of God?

A. That there is a great Being who made

the world and the whole universe out of nothing.

Q. What reason have we to believe in the existence of a Creator?

A. When we observe the strict order in which the world and all other planets move; the regular changes of time and seasons, and the unchangeable laws of nature, we must conclude that some great, intelligent Being has established and still regulates the whole system. [1]

Q. What do we mean by the revelation?

A. That God has made known his will to man by giving to us certain laws and rules for our conduct through life.

Q. What reason have we to believe that God has made known his will by a special revelation?

A. Seeing that God made the world and man, and gave us understanding and a will to

---

1. "Lift up your eyes on high, and behold who has created these things; he that brings out their host by number; he calls them all by name; from Him who is great in might and strong in power, not one fails." Isa. xl. 2-6.

act, it is reasonable to believe that he gave us also some rules to guide our conduct. [1]

Q. What is meant by future reward and punishment?

A. That our soul, which is the essence of our being, will enjoy great happiness or suffer much grief after we are dead.

Q. Why do we believe in a future recompense?

A. Because we often see good men suffer great misery in this world, while the wicked enjoy prosperity: we therefore believe that God, who is just, will fully reward every man hereafter. [2]

THIRD LESSON.

GOD'S ATTRIBUTES.

Q. Can we know anything about God except that he exists?

---

1. "See, I have taught you statutes and ordinances, as the Lord my God commanded me, * * * * * * keep therefore and do them, for this is your wisdom and your understanding." Deut. iv. 5-6.

2. "Far be it from God, that he should act wickedly, and from the Almighty to do wrong. For the work of a man shall he render unto him, and cause every man to find according to his ways." Job xxxiv. 10, 11.

A. Yes, we may know his qualities or attributes, from his works which we see.

Q. Which are the chief attributes of God, that exhibit themselves to us?

A. His power, wisdom, and goodness.

Q. Wherein can we see God's power?

A. When we think of the vast extent of God's creation, we are penetrated with a sense of that great power which made so many and such large bodies, and we say, God is All-Mighty! [1]

.Q. In what does God's wisdom show itself to us?

A. When we think of the beauties of Nature, and how all things work in order and agreement with one another, we are convinced of the wisdom of Him who made and who regulates it all, and we say, God is All-Wise! [2]

Q. Wherein can we see God's goodness?

A. When we observe how God gives life

—————

1. "The Heavens declare the glory of God; and the firmament tells of the works of his hands." Ps. xix. 1.

2. "How manifold are thy works, O Lord! In wisdom hast thou made them all. The earth is full of thy possessions." Ps. civ 24. Also, Prov. iii. 19; Jer. x. 3; and Job. xxxviii. 36.

and sustenance to all his creatures, providing for them what is necessary and suitable ; how he placed it in the nature of parents to love and provide for their children, we feel his goodness, and we say, God is All-Good. [3]

Q. What other attributes belong necessarily to the Divine Being ?

A. That he is spiritual, eternal, unchangeable and self-existing.

Q. What, then, must we conclude from the knowledge of these attributes of God ?

A. That he is the greatest and most perfect Being of which we can have any conception ; and that neither his being nor his workings can ever by us be perfectly understood, since his greatness and perfection are above our understanding.

FOURTH LESSON.

THE RELATION OF MAN TO GOD.

Q. In what relation do we stand to our Creator ?

---

3. " The Lord is good to all, and his mercies are over all his works." "The eyes of all wait upon thee, and thou givest them their food in due season. Thou openest thy hand, and satisfiest every living being with benevolence." Ps. cxlv. 9, 15, 16.

A. In the relation of subjects to a ruler and as children to their parents.[1]

Q. How can we be like children to God, since he is spiritual and holy, and we are human and sinful ?

A. It is our soul, which is also spiritual, and proceeding immediately from God, that gives us the quality of being like unto God.

Q. What does this relation between man and God imply ?

A. It implies that, as God rules over us like a sovereign and loves us like a parent, we in return owe him obedience and gratitude.

Q. In what does God's special love for man show itself ?

A. In that he made man superior to all other creatures by giving him reason and understanding, and the power to rule over all inferior beings. [2]

---

1. " The Lord is our judge, the Lord is our lawgiver, the Lord is our king, He will save us." Isaiah, xxxiii. 22. " As a father has mercy on his children, so has the Lord mercy on those that fear him." Ps. ciii. 13.

2. " Thou hast made him (man) but little less than a divine being, and hast crowned him with honor and glory.

Q. How should we acknowledge God as a superior ruler?

A. By observing his laws, submitting cheerfully to his decrees, receiving with patience and resignation even the severest visitations, under the conviction that they proceed from an all-wise Ruler.

Q. In what manner should we respect God as a Father?

A. By looking up to him with the highest veneration and love; thanking him for his favors; and by loving and respecting our fellow-creatures as children of the same universal parent.

FIFTH LESSON.

DOCTRINES OF THE JEWISH RELIGION.

Q. What does the Jewish religion teach particularly in regard to the existence of God?

A. That God is ONE, undivided and indivisible, and that there is no other divine being besides him.

Thou hast given him dominion over the works of thy hands; everything hast thou placed under his feet." Ps. viii. 5, 6.

Q. What reason have we for believing that there can be but ONE TRUE GOD?

A. When speaking of God, we think of him as the "FIRST CAUSE" of all that ever existed; and as *the first* can be but *one,* we must conclude that there can be but ONE TRUE GOD.

Q. What other reason have we to believe in God's absolute unity?

A. The Book of Revelation, in which we believe, teaches plainly that there is no other god, no other savior, and no other divine power but that great Being who revealed Himself to Moses. [1]

Q. What does the Jewish religion teach in regard to Revelation?

A. That God revealed Himself to Moses and the other prophets of the Bible, and that there is no divine revelation besides; and so it

---

1. "Hear, O Israel! The Lord, our God, is the ONE ETERNAL BEING." Deut. vi. 4. "See now that it is I, even I, and there is no god with me; I cause to die and I cause to live; I wound and I heal, and there is none that can deliver out of my hand." Deut. xxxii. 39. See also, Isa. xliii. 10-13, and xlv. 21, 22.

is declared in the Pentateuch, that if any prophet pretending to be sent from God should teach us different doctrine, we must reject him.[1]

Q. What doctrine do we hold in regard to future reward and punishment?

A. That the recompense of the soul will be of a purely spiritual nature; that it will have its reward in enjoying eternal life and bliss in the immediate presence of God, who is the source of life and of happiness, and its punishment in the opposite. [2]

SIXTH LESSON.

PRINCIPLES AND DUTIES.

Q. What constitutes a system of religion?

A. A system of religion consists of certain principles to be believed and certain duties to be performed.

---

1. "If there arise in thy midst a prophet, * * * * saying, let us go after other gods, which thou hast not known, and let us serve them; thou shalt not hearken unto the words of that prophet." Deut. xiii. 2, 3.

2. Thou wilt show me the path of life; in thy presence is fullness of joy; at thy right hand there are pleasures for evermore." Ps. xvi. 11.

Q. What do we understand by principles in religion ?

A. Certain opinions which, after due consideration and study, we accept as truths, and which form the foundation of our faith.

Q. And what is meant by religious duties ?

A. Certain acts which our religion requires us to perform ; and that it is also our duty to abstain from certain things which religion forbids us to do.

Q. What are the principles of the Jewish religion ?

A. God's absolute unity ; the truth and validity of the Mosaic laws and the prophetical writings ; the immortality of the soul ; and future reward and punishment.

Q. What are the chief duties required by our religion ?

A. The worship of the true God ; the observance of the Sabbath and Holidays ; justice and charity towards our fellow-beings ; and the promotion of the general welfare of mankind.

Q. Into how many and what classes may be divided all the duties we have to perform ?

A. Into three classes, namely : duties towards God ; duties towards our fellow-beings ; and duties towards ourselves.

Q. What are our duties towards God ?

A. To obey his will, to reverence and worship him, and to be thankful for his goodness.

Q. What are our duties towards our neighbors?

A. To be just and charitable ; to promote their morals and welfare ; and, in general, to do to them as we wish them to do to us.

Q. What duties are we to perform towards ourselves ?

A. To improve our mind and understanding ; to acquire knowledge ; and to watch over the preservation of our life and health.

Q. What are we to expect if we do our duties towards God and man ?

A. That God will bless us and make us happy here and hereafter.

Q. And what if we neglect those duties ?

A. That God will punish us and we will be miserable.

SEVENTH LESSON.

OF SIN AND REPENTANCE.

Q. What should be the great object of man's life and actions ?

A. To promote his own perfection and happiness, and at the same time that of his fellow-creatures.

Q. What are chiefly the means by which we may promote our perfection and happiness ?

A. First of all, to learn and seek the truth, in order to distinguish between right and wrong ; and next, to do what is good and abstain from evil.

Q. Why is it that we so often see man do what is wrong and evil, instead of promoting his own good ?

A. Partly from ignorance, and partly from man's natural inclination to sin.

Q. Did we not say that man is naturally inclined for religion ?

A. Yes, but man, being made of body and soul, is of a twofold nature. His soul, being God-like, is inclined to purely spiritual enjoyments, while his animal nature draws him to sensual pleasures and to sin.

Q. If our bodily nature inclines us to sin, why should we be punished for it ?

A. Because God has given us the power of reason to distinguish between right and wrong, and the power to control our inclination to sin. It is, therefore, both our duty and interest to choose the good and avoid the evil. [1]

Q. How can we best control our inclination to sin?

A. By endeavoring and habituating ourselves to do what is good; by frequently attending at the house of God to pray and listen to religious instruction; and by avoiding small transgressions, which are sure to lead to greater ones.

Q. Are we able then to escape entirely the influence of our sinful nature?

A. It is impossible for us entirely to overcome our natural infirmity, for even the best and greatest of men have sometimes sinned; but it is our duty to control our passions as much as we can. [2]

---

1. " I call heaven and earth as witness against you this day, that I have set before you life and death, blessing and cursing; therefore, choose thou life, that both thou and thy offspring may live." Deut. xxx. 19.

2. " Surely if thou doest well thou shalt be accepted, and if thou doest not well, sin lieth at the door, and unto thee is its desire, but thou canst rule over it." Gen. iv. 7.

Q. Have we any means to escape the punishment after we have sinned ?

A. If we see our error, feel sorry for what we have done, and determine to improve our conduct, God will forgive us; and he has even appointed the time and the means for us to obtain his pardon.

Q. Would not God's justice demand that the sinner be punished without remission ?

A. It is the peculiar attribute of the Divine Judge to temper justice with mercy: besides, repentance will restore us to purity and rectitude, and make us fit to deserve God's favor.

Q. But are we not taught in the Scriptures that to obtain pardon, we must offer sacrifices ?

A. Sacrifices were instituted only for our forefathers, who were addicted to idolatry, to draw them from their false worship and train them to the service of God;[1] but now our

---

1. "That the children of Israel may bring their sacrifices which they offer in the open field, that they may bring them unto the Lord, to the door of the tabernacle of the congregation. * * * * and they shall no more offer their sacrifices to the demons after which they have gone astray." Lev. xvii. 5. See also I Sam. xv. 22, and Isa. i. 10-17.

prayers take the place of sacrifices, for God desires only that our mind and heart be directed to him.[1]

EIGHTH LESSON.

THE BIBLE AND ITS DIVISIONS.

Q. What is the name of the book in which the laws and duties of our religion are prescribed ?

A. The Bible, or Holy Scriptures, commonly called the Old Testament.

Q. What are the principal divisions of the Bible ?

A. They are three : *first*, the Pentateuch, or Five Books of Moses ; *second*, the Prophets, and *third*, the Hagiographa, or sacred writings.

Q. How may the contents of the Pentateuch be divided ?

A. It contains, *first*, the history of the creation, of the patriarchs, of the formation of Israel as a distinct nation, and their subsequent history down to the death of their great leader

---

1. " Take with you words, and turn to the Lord ; say unto him, pardon all iniquity, and receive us graciously ; so will we replace the steers by (the prayers of) our lips." Hos. xiv. 3.

Moses ; and *second*, it contains laws and ordinances for the guidance of the Jewish people.

Q. How are the Mosaic laws to be divided ?

A. Into moral, sanitary and ceremonial laws.

Q. What is meant by moral laws ?

A. Such as are intended for the formation of man's character, and such as regard his conduct in relation to others—as the laws of loving God and our neighbor ; of honoring our parents and aged persons ; of justice, benevolence, etc.

Q. What are sanitary laws ?

A. Such as relate to the preservation of health : as the laws concerning forbidden food ; concerning cleanliness and purification, etc.

Q. What are ceremonial laws ?

A. Such as prescribe certain outward forms and rites to be observed as acts of religion : as the laws of blowing the cornet ; of eating unleavened bread ; of dwelling in the tabernacle, etc.

Q. How may the Mosaic laws be otherwise divided ?

A. Into positive and negative. Positive laws are those prescribing certain acts to be performed ; and negative laws are those forbidding certain acts to be done.

Q. Are those various laws all binding on us at the present time.

A. No ; a great many of them were intended only for former times, and for the country in which our ancestors lived ; many of them were instituted to eradicate idolatry. But those which were given to establish good morals, and others which relate to our national history, are to be observed by us at all times.

NINTH LESSON.

SUMMARY OF JEWISH DOCTRINE.

The principles and doctrines upon which the whole system of the Jewish religion is founded may be reduced to the following articles :

1st. That there exists ONE GOD, the undivided and indivisible Creator and Ruler of the universe, in whom is centered the essence of all power and wisdom and goodness.[1]

2d. That the omnipotent Creator rules the universe exclusively by his own dominion, and that no mediator of whatever nature is allowed to intervene between Him and His creatures.[2]

3d. That the Almighty God revealed his will and commandments to Moses and the whole nation of Israel, our ancestors. [3]

4th. That the writings of Moses and the prophets who succeeded him were written by divine authority and inspiration ; and that these only constitute the Holy Bible or Testament.[4]

5th. That the Bible, or Holy Scriptures, which we have now in our possession, contain the same laws which God delivered to Moses, and that these alone are the rule and guide for our religious conduct. [5]

6th. That the human soul—the essence of our being—is spiritual and immortal, like the Almighty God who gave it. [6]

7th. That our soul, after being by death separated from our body, will receive its reward or punishment at the hands of the Creator, in accordance with our acts and conduct in the present life. [7]

8th. That at some future period God will enlighten the understanding of all mankind, so that universal knowledge shall reign among them ; when all shall have the true faith and knowledge of God's indivisible Unity; when permanent peace and good will shall reign over all, and all peoples and nations enjoy the most perfect happiness attainable on earth. [8]

---

1. "Hear, O Israel! The Lord our God is the ONE ETERNAL BEING." Deut. vi. 4.

2. "Thus saith the Lord, the King of Israel, and his Redeemer, the Lord of hosts; I am the first and I am the last, and besides me there is no God." Isa. xliv. 6. "I, even I, am the Lord, and besides me there is no savior." Isa. xliii. 11.

3. "And the Lord said unto Moses, Lo! I come unto thee in a thick cloud, that the people may hear when I speak to thee, and believe also in thee forever." Ex. xix. 9.

4. "Thou didst admonish them by thy spirit through thy prophets." Neh. ix. 30.

6. "The dust shall return to the earth as it was, and the spirit shall return unto God who gave it." Ecc. xii. 7.

7. "God will bring every act into judgment, with every secret thing, whether it be good or evil." Ecc. xii. 14.

8. "The wolf shall lie down with the lamb, and the leopard shall lie down with the kid, and the calf and the young lion and the fatling together, and a little child shall lead them. They shall not hurt nor destroy in all my holy mountain, for the earth shall be full of the knowledge of the Lord, as the waters cover the sea." Isa. xi. 6 and 9. "And the Lord shall be King over all the earth; on that day the Lord shall be (acknowledged as) one, and his name shall be one "

SECOND PART.

PRACTICAL RELIGION.

TENTH LESSON.

PRAYER.

Q. What are the chief duties required by our religion?

A. The worship of the true God; the observance of the Sabbath and Holidays; justice and charity towards our fellow-beings; and the promotion of the general welfare of mankind.

Q. In what consists the worship of God?

A. In supremely reverencing and adoring him, and offering our prayers, thanks and praises to him?[1]

Q. Why should we adore and reverence God above all?

A. Because he is the most perfect Being, the author of our existence and our happiness, and the source of all that is good and holy.

---

1. " The Lord thy God shalt thou fear, and Him shalt thou serve." Deut. vi. 13.

Q. Why should we offer our thanks and praises to God ?

A. Because he gives us life and sustenance. The feeling of gratitude will prompt every good man to thank the one who gives him what he needs, and it were unnatural and wicked not to thank God for his goodness.

Q. What effect has the worship of God on ourselves ?

A. When we truly worship God, we are penetrated with a feeling of his constant presence ; we think of his greatness and goodness ; and our mind being thus impressed, our soul is ennobled, and we become more God-like.

Q. What is the utility of asking God for what we need, since he knows all our wants ?

A. It is not to inform God of our wants, nor to urge him to give us what we ask, but to remind us of our deficiency, and our dependence upon him for all that we enjoy.

Q. Why may we expect that God will grant our supplications when we pray to him ?

A. Not because we ask him, but because our calling upon him in sincerity and devotion shows such a disposition of heart as qualifies us to receive the divine favor.

Q. What things are absolutely necessary to make our prayers acceptable?

A. 1st, that we be impressed with a sense of God's greatness and our deficiency; 2d, that we thoroughly understand what we say; and 3d, that we feel the importance of what we say.

Q. In what different ways may we worship God?

A. We may worship him in private or in public.

Q. What times are most suitable for private prayer?

A. At night, before we retire; in the morning, after rising; and after our meals.

Q. What times are most suitable for public prayer?

A. Sabbaths and Holidays.

Q. What advantage is there in assembling for public worship?

A. When we meet together for the purpose of praying, at stated times, and at the house dedicated for that particular object, it increases our devotion ; besides, we receive religious instruction and exhortation there.

Q. Is it necessary that we should always express our prayers in words ?

A. No. Since God knows our feelings, we may be engaged in prayer even in silence ; especially when we join with devotion in the prayers recited for us. · ˙

Q. What ought to be the principal subjects of our regular prayers ?

A. We should pray God to assist us in being good and virtuous, to pardon our sins, and to give us our daily wants ; and it is proper also that we should pray for the good of others.

Q. Why should we not despair or lose confidence when we do not see our prayers answered ?

A. Because we are often ignorant of what is good for us. If God does not grant what we ask, we should confide in his wisdom and goodness, and trust that he will give us something that is really better for us.

ELEVENTH LESSON.

SABBBATH AND FESTIVALS.

Q.   Which are the days of rest and festivals observed in our religion ?

A.   The weekly Sabbath,—the Passover, or feast of unleavened bread,—the Pentecost, or feast of weeks,—the Feast of Tabernacles, including the Atsereth,—the Day of Memorial, or New Year's Day,—and the Day of Atonement.

Q.   What is the object of the Sabbath institution ?

A.   That we should call to mind that God is the Creator and Ruler of the Universe, wherefore we owe him reverence and obedience ; and to teach us that, as the days of labor are followed by a day of rest, so may we, after having duly performed our earthly toil, enjoy eternal rest and felicity.

Q.   How is the Sabbath to be kept ?

A.   We must " remember the Sabbath-day to keep it holy," and " do no servile work thereon ; " that is, we must set it apart for divine worship, and not attend to our daily vocations or worldly pursuits of either business or pleasure.

Q. In what cases are we permitted to do labor on the Sabbath?

A. We may do all that is necessary for the preservation of life, or to relieve the sick and suffering; also, we may impart religious instruction, and do all that is immediately connected with divine worship.

Q. What is the object of the Passover celebration?

A. We celebrate the redemption of our forefathers from Egyptian bondage; the day when we were made a distinct nation, chosen by God to be his ministers among mankind.

Q. What moral lesson may we derive from the observance of the Passover?

A. It teaches us that God, who delivered us and punished our oppressors, is the supreme Governor and Judge of the world, who protects the innocent and punishes the wicked.

Q. What particular ceremonies are connected with the Passover?

A. It is customary that, on the first night, the members of every Jewish family assemble

in devotion for the recital of the history of the
exodus ; partaking of the unleavened bread
and bitter herbs, which remind us of the cir-
cumstances which attended the mighty delivery
wrought for our ancestors ; while the use of all
things leavened is forbidden during the seven
days.

Q. Why do we observe the feast of Pentecost ?

A. It was originally instituted to offer at
the temple in Jerusalem two measures of fine
flour at the conclusion of the wheat harvest.
This ceremony has ceased for us, but we now
celebrate the delivery of the Ten Commandments on Mount Sinai, which took place at the
same date.

Q. What is the observance of this festival
intended to teach us ?

A. It is intended to teach us this great
truth : that God has instructed man by a special
revelation, and that we Israelites are made the
keepers and guardians of the laws of God, and
chosen by him to stand before the world as

teachers of his laws, and as an example in their observance.[1]

Q. What correspondence is there between the former celebration of the harvest-feast and the present observance of the Pentecost ?

A. The feast of the harvest was to remind the people that God gives nourishment to all his creatures; while now, the remembrance of the Revelation teaches us that God supplies us also with spiritual food, which is the richest harvest we can gather.

Q. What is the origin of the feast of Tabernacles ?

A. It was instituted as a feast of rejoicing and thanksgiving over the gathering of the fruits of trees and other productions of the soil, which in the Holy Land are gathered in at that season.

Q. What historical event does it commemorate ?

---

1. "Remember these things, O Jacob and Israel ! for thou art my servant. I have formed thee to be my servant; thou, Israel, must not forget me." Isa. xliv. 21. "Ye shall be called the priests of the Lord; 'Ministers of our God' shall be said unto you." Isa. lxi. 6.

A. It commemorates the mercy of God in providing our forefathers with booths or tents, while they lived in the wilderness, after they had gone out from Egypt.

Q. What particular ceremonies are connected with this festival?

A. We are commanded to take on the first day some beautiful fruit, with branches of the palm-tree and of certain other trees, and use them during divine service; and to live in tents during the seven days of the feast.

Q. What moral lesson does the observance of this festival teach us?

A. It reminds us that our stay on earth is but temporary. As we leave our regular houses to sit in tents, so we must once leave this world to rest in the grave.

Q. What is the feast of *Atsereth?*

A. It is the concluding festival of the Tabernacles, though not to be kept with the same ceremonies. It is of equal importance as a holiday, and celebrated by the annual or triennial finishing and re-commencing of the public reading of the law. It is, therefore, called also

Simchath Torah, i. e., feast of rejoicing with the law.

Q. What is the general character and manner of observance of the three festivals?

A. They are to be devoted partly to divine service and partly to domestic enjoyment ; no labor is to be performed except what is necessary in preparing our food.

Q. What striking difference is there between the manner of observance of the Jewish festivals and that in which other nations observed theirs ?

A. Among the ancients, public festivals were generally connected with idolatry, superstition and folly, and celebrated with games and theatrical performances. At a later period they were accompanied with the grossest vices and immoralities ; and even at the present time, ·public holidays are often devoted to intemperance and dissipation ; while our festivals are all kept in commemoration of some historical events, connected with the most ·solemn duties of religion, and their general tendency is to improve our morals.

TWELFTH LESSON.

DAY OF MEMORIAL, DAY OF ATONEMENT, AND POST-MOSAIC FESTIVALS.

Q. What is the origin of the Day of Memorial, or New Year's Day?

.A. The reason for observing this holiday is not explained in the Bible, but it is ordered to be kept as a " day of memorial, of blowing the trumpets."

Q. What may the blowing of trumpets on that day signify?

A. It should serve as a warning to prepare ourselves for the great Day of Atonement, which occurs a few days afterwards.

Q. Why is that day fixed upon as a New Year's Day?

A. It is supposed to be the anniversary of the world's creation, and, as such, it is naturally considered the beginning of the year, though at the deliverance of Israel from Egypt the month Nissan was instituted to be accounted the first month of the year in commemoration of the great event.

Q. For what purpose was the Day of Atonement instituted?

A. The Day of Atonement has been appointed by God in mercy to his people, that we should seriously reflect on our conduct during the past year, repent of our sins, and obtain pardon from our gracious Father in heaven.

Q. How is the day to be observed?

A. We should humble ourselves before our Creator, praying for his forgiveness, and resolving to better our conduct; and we should fast and abstain from all worldly enjoyments, from sunset on the previous day till the evening of the day itself.

Q. Why should we abstain from all food and drink on that day?

A. Because by fasting we are made to feel our weakness; our pride is humbled, and we feel the more our dependence on God as the giver of all.

Q. Why should this day be set apart for duties which we may perform on any day?

A. It is necessary that some day should be appointed for particular humiliation and prayer, for that which may be done at any time we are apt to put off till it is too late.

Q. What festivals are to be observed which are not ordained in the Mosaic laws ?

A. The *Hannukah* and *Purim.*

Q. What event do we celebrate on the Hannukah festival ?

A. We celebrate the victory which, by the providential direction of God, our forefathers gained under Judas Maccabæus, who delivered his people from the oppression of the Syrian king Antiochus, and restored the divine service to the temple which had been desecrated.

Q. How is the *Hannukah* celebrated ?

A. By the recital of certain appropriate prayers and hymns, and the lighting of extra lamps in our synagogues and dwellings, the same as our forefathers did when they again dedicated the temple. (Hannukah means dedication.)

Q. What is the origin of the Purim festival ?

A. The deliverance which God granted to our nation, by means of Mordechai and Esther, from the destruction which the wicked Haman had designed against our forefathers who lived in Persia.

Q. How is it celebrated ?

A. By the public reading of the Book of Esther, which contains the whole history of the Purim; the offering of additional prayers and thanks to God; the distribution of presents to our friends, and alms to the needy; and by social festivities.

Q. Why is it called Purim?

A. Purim means *lots*, and the festival is so called because Haman determined by lot the day on which he intended to destroy his enemies.

Q. What is the character of these Post-Mosaic festivals?

A. They are not holidays, but merely days of national festivity; and after the religious services held on them, they are devoted to social enjoyment, and labor is not forbidden.

THIRTEENTH LESSON.

THE JEWISH CALENDER.

Q. How is the Jewish year divided?

A. Into twelve months, of twenty-nine or thirty days each; and thirteen months in leap year.

Q. How often does leap-year occur?

A. Seven times in every nineteen years; that is, nearly every third year.

Q. What are the names of the Hebrew months?

A. Nissan, Iyar, Sivan, Tammuz, Ab, Elul, Tishri, Heshvan, Kislev, Tebeth, Shebat Addar and Addar Sheni, or Second Addar in leap-year.

Q. By what are the Hebrew months regulated?

A. By the re-appearance of the moon, which happens at intervals of twenty-nine and a half days and some minutes.

Q. What do we call the day of the new appearance of the moon?

A. *Rosh Hodesh,* or new moon's day.

Q. How is it observed?

A. Anciently, in the time of the temple service, it was observed partly as a holiday; but it is now remembered only by some additional portions in our prayers, and announced on the Sabbath preceding it.

Q. Do we at present fix the new moon's day by the re-appearance of that orb?

A. No; formerly the day was so fixed at Jerusalem, upon the declaration of witnesses having stated that they had seen the first phasis on a certain day and hour. But since the Jewish calender has been accurately computed, the exact days of *Rosh Hodesh* have been fixed upon for all future time.

Q. How was the new moon's day then announced to the public?

A. It was publicly proclaimed in Jerusalem, and messengers were sent through the country to announce the day which had been appointed, that the people might know when to observe the holidays.

Q. What was the consequence and disadvantage of fixing the *Rosh Hodesh* by the appearance of the moon?

A. That many persons who were at a great distance from Jerusalem, where the messengers could not reach in time, did not know exactly the day of the month, and were, therefore, obliged to keep two holidays instead of one.

Q. Why do some Jewish congregations at present observe two successive holidays each time?

A. Because it was kept so by some of our ancestors, who were in doubt, as we have just said.

Q.   Are then the second days not kept holy by all Jewish communities ?

A.   No : in the Holy Land they were never so observed, and are not at the present day ; and many other congregations have discarded them as unnecessary and superfluous.

Q.   In what month and on what day does the Passover occur ?

A.   The fourteenth of Nissan is properly the Passover feast, because on that day the paschal lamb was to be offered ; but the feast of unleavened bread begins on the fifteenth and lasts seven days.

Q.   Which of these are to be observed as holidays ?

A.   The first and the seventh.

Q.   When is the Pentecost celebrated ?

A.   On the sixth day of the month Sivan ; that is, fifty days after the first of Passover. Pentecost means fiftieth.   It is also called *the feast of weeks*, because seven weeks exactly elapse between the two festivals.

Q.   When are the feasts of Tabernacles and Atsereth observed ?

A.   The feast of Tabernacles begins on the

fifteenth of *Tishri*, and lasts seven days, but only the first is a holiday. The eighth, i. e., the twenty-second of the month, is Atsereth, which means concluding festival.

Q. When do the New Year's Day and Day of Atonement occur?

A. The New Year's Day is on the first of *Tishri*, and the Day of Atonement on the tenth of the same month.*

Q. On what date does the *Hannukah* happen?

A. It begins on the twenty-fifth of *Kislev*, and continues for eight days.

Q. When is the *Purim* festival kept?

A. On the fourteenth of *Addar*, and in some places of the Orient on the fifteenth. In leap-year it is kept on the same days in the second *Addar*.

FOURTEENTH LESSON.

SANITARY AND MORAL LAWS.

Q. What are sanitary laws?

A. Such as relate to the preservation of

*For ordinances regarding the festivals see Lev. xxxiii.

health : as the laws concerning forbidden food ; concerning cleanliness and purification, etc.

Q. What kinds of food are forbidden ?

A. The flesh of certain animals enumerated in the eleventh chapter of Leviticus; blood drawn from the animal ;[1] certain parts of the fat of cattle ;[2] and the flesh of an animal that died from disease,[3] or was killed by a ferocious beast.[4]

Q. What reason may be given for the prohibition of these things ?

A. That they are generally unwholesome, and particularly so in hot climates, such as our forefathers lived in.

Q. What other sanitary laws do we find in the Mosaic code ?

A. Regulations for cleanliness of our person, such as frequent washing and bathing, which is especially necessary in hot countries ; also preventives against certain diseases which are prevalent in warm climates.

Q. What general principle may we learn from these laws ?

---

1. Lev. vii. 26.   2. Lev. vii. 23.   3. Deut. xiv. 20.
4. Ex. xxii. 30.   See also Lev. xvii. 10–16.

A. That it is man's duty to preserve and promote his health, so that he may be able to perform his duties towards God, his neighbor, and himself.

Q. How should this principle be particularly applied to our mode of living?

A. That we should moderate the indulgence of our appetites and passions; avoid all excess in eating and drinking, and never gratify our desires to their fullest extent; for the immoderate use of anything that is good brings on satiety and disgust.

Q. What is meant by moral laws?

A. Such as are intended for the formation of man's character, and such as regard his conduct in relation to others: as the laws of loving God and our neighbor; of honoring our parents and aged persons; of justice and charity, etc.

Q. What two sentences of the Scriptures can you name which comprise all the moral duties we have to perform?

A. One is, " Thou shalt love the Lord thy God with all thy heart, and with all thy soul, and with all thy might "; and the other, " Thou shalt love thy neighbor like thyself."

Q. How do these short sentences express all our moral obligations ?

A. If we truly love God, because we are convinced of his greatness and goodness, we shall certainly obey his will; and if we love our fellow-beings, we cannot injure them, but will surely do all we can to promote their welfare.

Q. What duty is next in importance to that of loving God ?

A. The love and respect which we owe our parents. This duty is of such great importance that it has been ranked among the Ten Commandments, in which only the chief duties of man are prescribed. [1]

Q. Why is the duty of love and respect to parents of such great importance ?

A. Because it lays the foundation in forming our character when young. Our parents are our best friends, and being older and wiser than ourselves, they direct us for our best, and if we follow them, we shall certainly do well when grown up.

---

1. " Honor thy father and thy mother, that thy days may be long in the land that the Lord thy God gives thee."

Q. When the Scripture says, "honor thy father and thy mother," does it mean that we should pay them respect in their presence only?

A. No: it means that we should obey their commands at all times, and act according to their wishes, even if they do not express them, for their wishes are all for our happiness.

Q. What result does experience show us in regard to this duty?

A. It has been generally observed that the best and greatest of men have been obedient and respectful children; while many criminals have confessed that their disobedience to parents was the source of all their crimes and misfortunes.

Q. Who are next entitled to our respect and obedience?

A. Our teachers, both private and public, and the magistrates of the government under which we live.[1] We owe reverence also to aged persons,[2] and must show respect and politeness towards all men, even to our inferiors.

---

1. "Thou shalt go to the priests, the Levites and the judge that shall be in those days, and inquire, and they shall tell thee the judgment. * * According to the law

FIFTEENTH LESSON.

MORAL LAWS — CONTINUED.

Q. What other moral ordinances besides those mentioned in the preceding lesson are prominent in the Books of Moses ?

A. Those which ordain us to be just, charitable, truthful and forgiving towards our fellow beings.

Q. Name some particular instances where the law commands us to be just.

A. In general it says, " Justice, justice, shalt thou follow, that thou mayest live. " (Deut. xvi. 20.) We are forbidden not only to steal, but to commit any kind of fraud in weights, measures or otherwise ; to take a bribe or usury ; to retain the wages of a hired person over night ; to take in pledge any garment or tool which a poor owner may need ; we must restore any lost object we find, and many other instances.

Q. Is it only in the immediate acts of taking

which they shall teach thee, thou shalt do, * * thou shalt not deviate to the right nor to the left." Deut. xvii. 9–11.

2. " Thou shalt rise before the hoary head, and honor the presence of the old man." Lev. xix. 32.

or retaining possession of what is not rightly our own that we can be unjust?

A. No: we sin against the laws of justice when we deceive others; if in selling and buying we represent things different from what they are; or if we agree to work for certain wages and do not employ our time as agreed upon, and in other similar ways.

Q. Can we commit any act of injustice where neither money nor property is concerned?

A. We commit great injustice when we injure any person's character; when we invent or circulate false tales to deprive him of his good name.

Q. What special command does the law give on this subject?

A. It says, " Thou shalt not pronounce a false report," (Ex. xxiii. 1) and in another place, " Thou shalt not go about as a tale-bearer among thy people." (Lev. xix. 16.)

Q. When we know in truth anything that is wrong about our neighbor, are we at liberty to expose him?

A. Not unless we have very good reason to do so. We should remember that we are all sinners ; we all have our failings, and therefore should be kind and generous in our sentiments, as well as honest in our dealings.

Q. What, then, is the general principle of justice which should guide us in all our acts towards a fellow-being ?

A. We should be guided by the great rule of " loving our neighbor like ourselves," that is, treating others as we wish to be treated by them.

Q. What other injury can we do our neighbor besides depriving him of his property or good name ?

A. The greatest injury we can do to others is to tempt or induce them to do what is wrong. If we take their property, they may recover it; if we deprive them of their good name, they may regain it ; but if we attack their virtue and conscience, we put them in danger of losing forever the best things they have.

Q. What special command does the Mosaic law give on this subject ?

A. It says, " Thou shalt not put a stumbling-block before the blind ; " (Lev. xix. 14.) that means, if one does not clearly see what is wrong, he is like blind to it, and if we tempt him we put a stumbling-block before him that he may fall into sin.

Q.   What is the meaning of charity?

A.   In a particular sense it means alms given to the poor; in a general sense it means that disposition of heart which inclines us to think and judge favorably of others.

Q.   Does the law command us to practice charity in both these senses?

A.   It does.   The latter sense of it is fully expressed in the command of "loving our neighbor"; and in regard to supporting and assisting the poor, the precepts are very plain and frequently repeated.[1]

Q.   In what manner should we give assistance to the poor?

A.   We should give it cheerfully and liberally; not with indifference, nor to relieve ourselves of the importunity of the applicant, nor in a manner that hurts his feelings; but with

---

1. "Thou shalt open thy hand widely to thy poor brethren, and to the needy in thy land." Deut. xv. 11. "Blessed is he who considers the poor; the Lord will deliver in time of trouble." Ps. xli. 1.

an open heart and free hand, and with gratitude to God who enables us to give.

Q. Name some particular commands found in the Mosaic law regarding charity to the poor.

A. In mowing the grain off the field, we are to leave a portion of it untouched that the poor may take it; sheaves that are forgotten, or single ears dropped on the field must be left for them; also certain parts of the vineyards and of other trees; in dismissing a servant we are to load him with gifts, and many similar commands are prescribed.

Q. What general rule may we learn from these commands?

A. They teach us that in giving to the poor we must do it in a manner which does not make them feel their poverty; looking upon them as our equals, less favored by divine Providence.

Q. Is truthfulness commanded and falsehood considered a sin by our law?

A. Truthfulness is frequently commanded us,[1] especially when giving evidence before

---

1. "Lying lips are an abomination to the Lord; but they that deal truly are his delight." Prov. xii. 22.

judges. In general it says, " ye shall not deal falsely, and ye shall not lie to one another." (Lev. x. 11.)

Q. Why is it a great sin to speak falsehood ?

A. Because falsehood destroys mutual confidence and social happiness. If we do not adhere to the truth, no one can depend upon us ; we deceive others, and must expect to be deceived in return.

Q. How should we feel and act towards persons who have injured or offended us ?

A. We should forgive others as well as we wish our sins and offences to be forgiven. It is very sinful to be unforgiving and revengeful.[1]

Q. What command does the Holy Scripture give us on that subject.

A. It says, " thou shalt not hate thy brother in thy heart"; (Lev. xix. 17.) and " thou shalt not avenge, nor bear any grudge against the children of thy people." (Lev. xix. 20.)

Q. Name some of the striking examples of forgiveness found in the Scriptures.

---

1. " Say not, 'as he has done to me, so will I do to him ; I will render to the man according to his work.' " Prov. xxiv. 29. " Say not, ' I will return evil; ' trust to the Lord, and he will help thee." Prov. xx. 22.

A. When Miriam had spoken maliciously of her brother Moses, and was punished for it with leprosy, he prayed God that she might be healed; and David forgave several times his deadly enemy Saul, who sought to take his life.

Q. What is it that causes man to be often unforgiving and revengeful?

A. It is a spirit of haughtiness and selfishness which makes us think too much of ourselves and too little of others. It is self-conceit which makes us angry and excited even at small and sometimes imaginary offences.

Q. What spirit should we endeavor to acquire and cultivate?

A. That of meekness and humility; we must endeavor to check angry feelings and control our temper. Moses, who is described as the greatest of prophets, was more humble and meek than any other man. (Num. xii. 3.)

Q. What short sentence do we find in the Bible which may serve as a safe guide in all our moral and religius acts?

A. That of the prophet Micah, who says: "He has told thee, O man! what isgood, and what the Lord required of thee: to do justice, to love kindness, and to walk humbly with thy God."

www.ingramcontent.com/pod-product-compliance
Lightning Source LLC
Chambersburg PA
CBHW031756090426
42739CB00008B/1033